SPEEDY MACHINES
BIKES

Vic Parker
Illustrated by Tom Connell

Belitha Press

First published in the UK in 1999 by
Belitha Press Limited
London House, Great Eastern Wharf
Parkgate Road, London SW11 4NQ

ISBN 1 84138 008 3

British Library Cataloguing in Publication Data for this book
is available from the British Library.

Printed in Singapore

Editor: Stephanie Bellwood
Designer: Helen James
Illustrator: Tom Connell
Consultant: Margaret Bellwood

Contents

Racing machines

All fast machines are noisy and exciting, from roaring racing cars to soaring planes and zooming powerboats. The drivers control them from a cabin or a cockpit. Motorbikes are different. The dare-devil riders sit on top of their machines with only their skill and strength to protect them. This book tells you about the powerful motorbikes they drive.

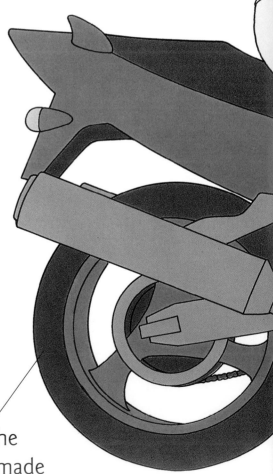

4

The **tyres** of the motorbike are made of tough rubber.

Riders wear **helmets** to protect their heads in case they crash. They also wear **padded clothing** to cushion them if they fall.

The bike's **control panel** shows information such as how fast the bike is moving and how much fuel is left.

There are **lights** on the front of the bike for riding at night.

The **engine** and the mechanical parts of the bike are covered by a smooth case called the **fairing.**

Speed stars

Motorbike races are almost too fast to see. The speediest bikes shoot along at 320 km/h or more. They follow each other closely as they chase down the straight parts of the track. When a bike catches up with the leader, it swerves out and overtakes as they whizz round a bend. Then everyone dashes for the finish!

Fast facts

Grand Prix bikes are built carefully by hand, just like racing cars. Engineers check and adjust every little part of the machines before a race.

6

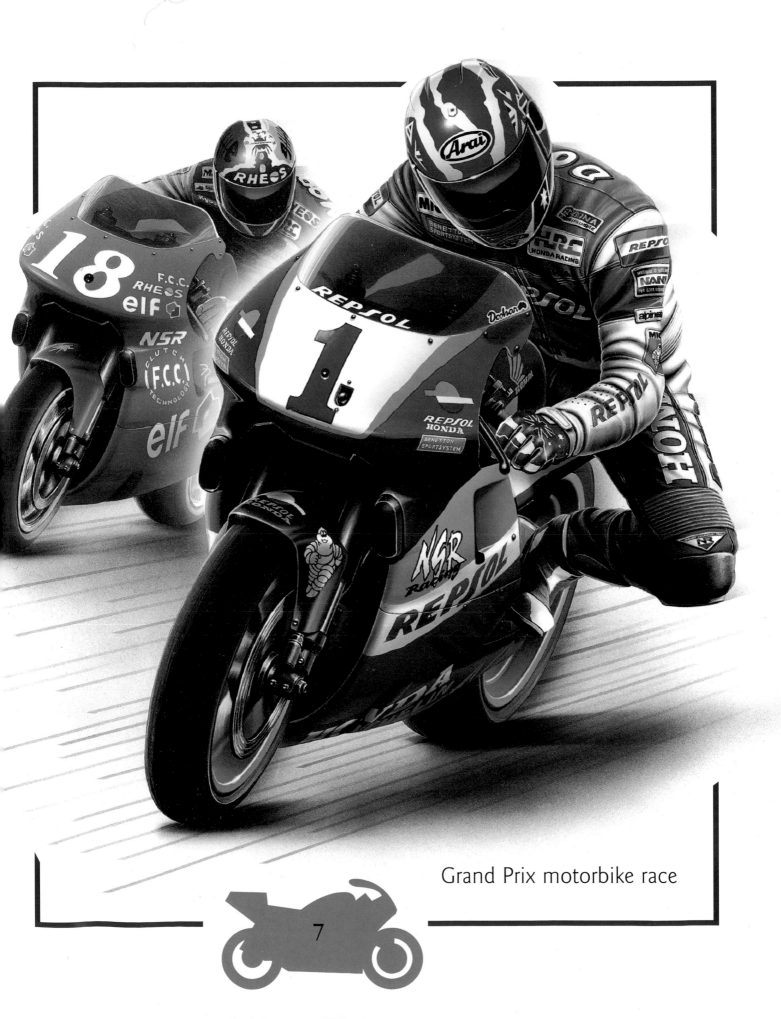

Grand Prix motorbike race

7

Built for speed

Fast motorbikes are light and strong with powerful engines. They are also thin and smooth to cut through the air easily. Even riders are part of this neat shape as they sit in long, low seats. Many motorbike fans love this Honda *Fireblade*. It can zoom along at 265 km/h.

Fast facts

The first motorbike was built in 1885 and had wooden wheels. It wasn't very comfortable to ride! The air-filled rubber tyres used today were invented in 1888.

Honda *Fireblade*

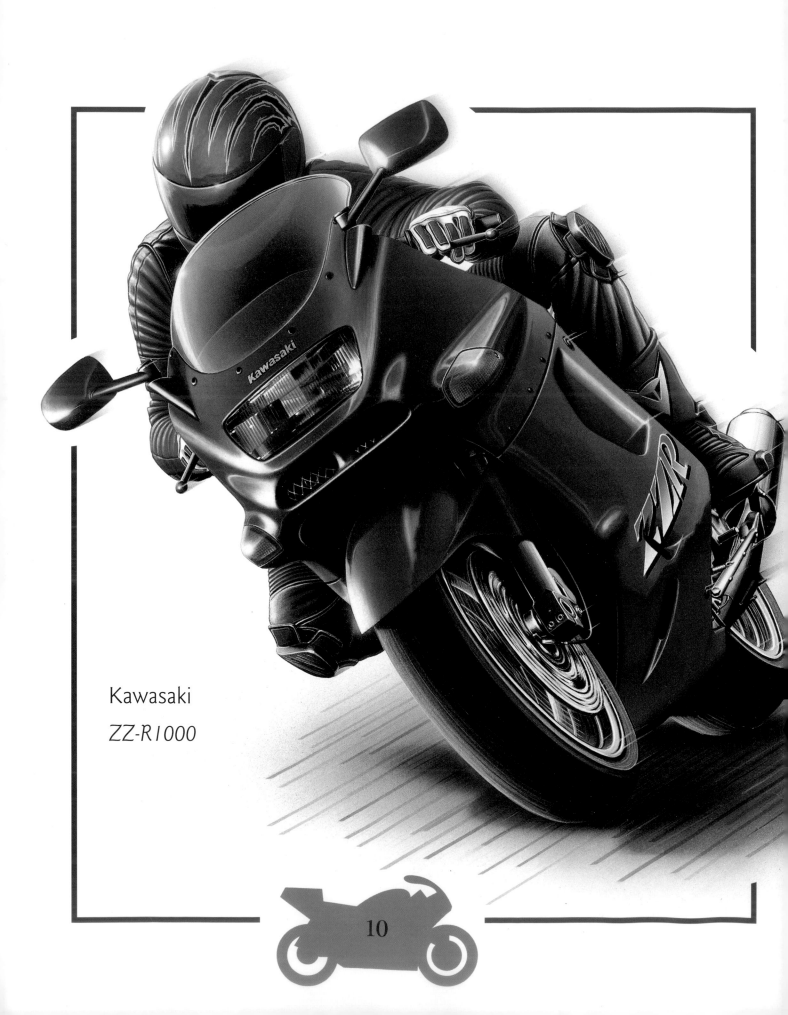

Kawasaki
ZZ-R1000

10

King of the road

The Kawasaki *ZZ-R1000* is one of the fastest road bikes in the world. Its engine runs on petrol like a car. Some racing machines burn a special fuel that makes them go even faster. A few bikes use jet engines like fighter planes. A stream of fiery gas shoots out as the bike zooms forwards, while the rider clings on as tightly as possible!

Fast facts

Some bikes carry a can of special booster gas. The rider presses a control that sprays the gas into the engine to give the bike an extra burst of speed.

11

Staying in control

If you've learned to ride a bicycle you'll know how tricky it is to stay up on two wheels. So imagine how difficult it is for a motorbike to turn corners at top speeds. Riders work hard in a race to stay in control of their bikes. They hang right off the sides to stay balanced – sometimes they lean over so far that their knees scrape the ground.

Fast facts

Racing motorbikes often have fatter tyres than ordinary bikes. These big, wide tyres can grip the track much better.

12

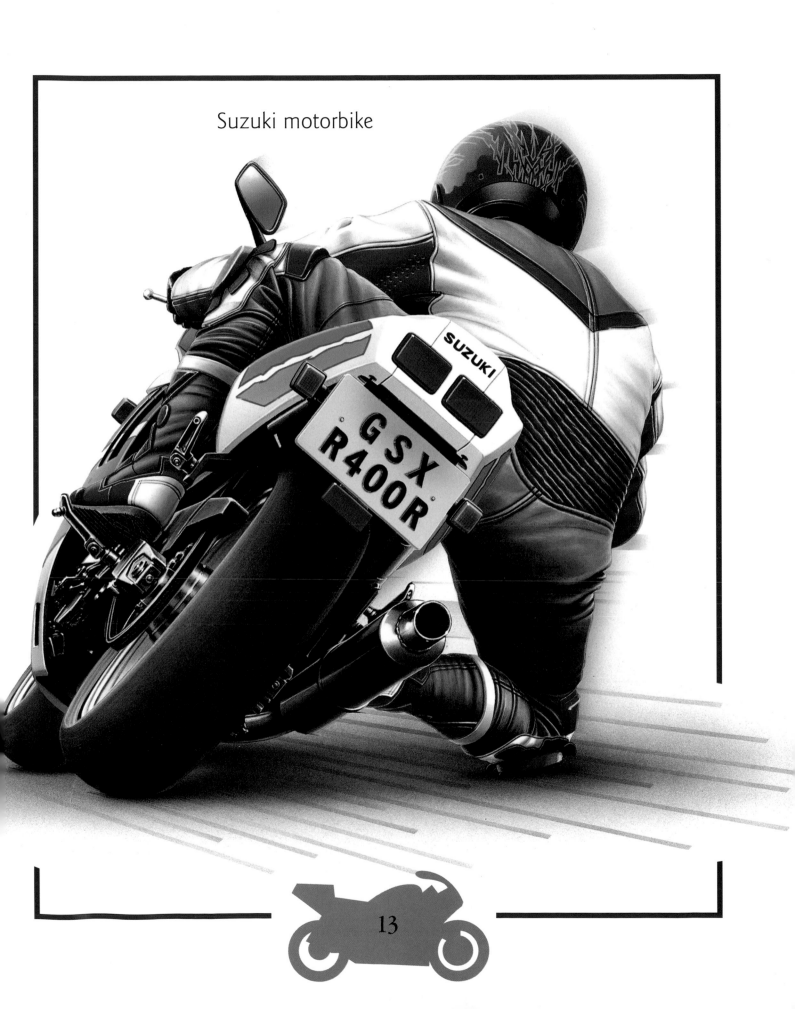

Suzuki motorbike

Kawasaki *ZX-9R*

14

Superbike superheroes

Superbikes are road machines that are light and slim like racing bikes. They are very powerful, stylish, popular and extremely expensive. Superbikes can reach speeds of more than 250 km/h, but they're not allowed to travel this fast on ordinary roads!

Fast facts

Superbikes are the fastest road bikes, but they are not the biggest. The largest, heaviest bikes on the road are called muscle bikes because of their enormous bulging engines.

Peak performance

If you want to see just how fast the speediest road machines can go, visit a superbike race. Watch out for the coloured flags that give riders important messages as they flash round the track. Yellow warns of danger ahead and red means that the race has been stopped. See if you can spot a Ducati *916*. It's one of the most famous superbikes in the world.

Fast facts

A superbike's engine has so much power that the front wheel sometimes lifts up off the ground as the bike speeds up. This is called pulling a wheelie.

16

Ducati 916

Off-road riding

Not all motorbikes ride on roads or racetracks. Motocross races take place across hilly countryside in all kinds of weather. This kind of racing is bumpy, dirty and tough! Motocross bikes are springy to help them bounce over humps and slide down slopes. Riders wear plastic vests called body armour because they fall off their bikes so often.

Fast facts

American hill-climbing is a sport in which motorbikes race up a very steep slope. Sometimes no-one is able to reach the top, so the one who climbs highest is the winner.

18

Motocross bike

Track stars

Speedway is another thrilling off-road motorbike sport. It's very dangerous. The racers slip and slide around rough dirt tracks on specially-designed bikes that don't have gears or brakes. The riders slam their feet down in the dirt to stay in control. Their machines skid round tight corners, sending up sprays of mud.

Fast facts

Speedway races can be held on ice. Ice bikes have tyres covered with long spikes for extra grip on the slippery surfaces.

Speedway bikes

Drag racing

Dragsters are among the most powerful motorbikes in the world. They're so quick that races only last around seven seconds – faster than the time it takes you to read this sentence. Just before the race starts, the bikes stand still and spin their wheels at high speed. Then they burst away, shooting like rockets down a short, straight track called a drag strip.

22

Fast facts

A dragster is weighted down at the back by a metal frame with wheels called a wheelie bar. It stops the bike pulling a huge wheelie and flipping over backwards.

drag bike

Triumph *T595 Daytona*

24

Motorbike style

People enjoy motorbikes not just because they are fast and exciting, but because they are stylish too. Some bikes gleam with many colours and others have a silvery shine. Riders often dress to match in bright bodysuits or bold black leathers. Engineers work hard to design stunning new motorbikes like this golden Triumph *T595 Daytona*.

Fast facts

Not all stylish bikes have a modern look. Some of the most beautiful bikes are old-fashioned, such as Harley Davidsons.

25

Safety tests

Every new motorbike design is carefully tested to make sure that it is safe. A rider sits on a model of the bike in a special tunnel. Air is blasted past the bike at high speeds and motorbike experts check that parts of the bike don't bend or break. It is very important that the real bike won't fall apart when it's racing along at speeds faster than 300 km/h!

Fast facts

Motorbike helmets might soon be fitted with air bags, like those in cars. In a crash, a bag pops out of the helmet and blows up around the rider's neck, protecting it like a cushion.

Honda motorbike model

Record breakers

Record-breaking bikes look like bullets. The rider and the body of the bike are covered by a long, slim tube. This makes the bike so smooth and speedy that it goes like a bullet too! In 1978 a bike called *Lightning Bolt* set a world speed record of 512 km/h. This record was unbeaten until 1990, when a machine called *Easyriders* reached 518 km/h.

Lightning Bolt

Shaping the future

Bike builders often experiment with modern technology and new designs by building a concept bike. These exciting test machines allow them to try out wild new ideas. The bikes look amazing and they also give us an idea of how motorbikes could look in the future. You might see this new Australian superbike on the roads in a few years' time. It will be able to travel faster than some sports cars.

30

Fast facts

Some bikes are made specially for riding in cities. They are small and light so they can nip through traffic, then speed away when they reach the open road.

Hunwick Hallum superbike

Index